THE LITTLE HOMELAND OF

John Paul II

27
YEARS
OF PONTIFICATE

SANTO SUBITO!

THE LITTLE HOMELAND OF
John Paul II

Adam Bujak

Kompozycja graficzna i redakcja
Leszek Sosnowski

CONTENTS

WADOWICE TIMES

1920	
May 18	KAROL JÓZEF WOJTYŁA is born in Wadowice to Karol and Emilia (born Kaczorowska) living at Rynek 2, apt. 4 – today, Kościelna 7.
June 20	He is baptized at the parish church by father Franciszek Żak – an army chaplain. Godparents: Józef Kuczmierczyk, the mother's brother-in-law, and Maria Wiadrowska, the mother's sister.
1926	
September 15	Karol begins to attend the local elementary school for boys.
1929	
April 13	Karol's mother dies following a short illness. She is later exhumed and reburied in the family grave at the Cracow military cemetery, where the Pope's father and brother are also buried.
May 25	First Holy Communion
1930	
May 26	Trip to Wieliczka, along with His father, teachers and schoolmates.
May 28	Trip to Cracow: the 10 year-old Karol participates in the Doctor of Medicine promotion ceremony of his brother Edmund, at the Jagiellonian University. While still attending elementary school, he takes part in a pilgrimage to Jasna Góra, together with his father and a group of friends.
September	Karol begins first grade at the Marcin Wadowita State Grammar School for Boys on Mickiewicz St. in Wadowice. He starts studying German – language his father began teaching him before. His farther has also put together a Polish-German dictionary for the boy.
1931	
June 27	He completes the first grade with neoclassical concentration. His overall grade – excellent. Excellent in all subjects.
1932	
June	He completes the second grade. Excellent grades in all subjects. His Polish Language grade bears an additional comment: "exhibits particular passion".
Summer	Participates in his parish's pilgrimage to Jasna Góra.
December 5	Karol's brother, Edmund dies. He was a physician at the City Hospital in Bielsko, where he died after contracting scarlet fever from a female patient during the epidemic of this disease.
1933	
August 10	The parish church bids farewell to the curate and religion teacher, father Kazimierz Figlewicz, who is moving to Cracow. After the Mass, Karol Wojtyła says the farewells on behalf of the altar boys.
1935	
November 9	School theatre production of *Antygona*. Karol Wojtyła played Haymon, something he recounts in Wadowice during his 1979 Papal visit – even reciting part of the role.
December 14	He is accepted to the Marian Sodality.
1936	
February	He begins an intense cooperation with the avant-garde theatrical director Mieczysław Kotlarczyk, who taught at a private school, ran by the Discalced

	Carmelite Friars. They spend hours discussing theatre, literature and philosophy.
February 29	The school theatre puts on the *Śluby panieńskie* (*Spinster Vows*) play. Karol Wojtyła plays Gucio.
April 26	He is chosen the Marian Sodality chairman of the students of the Marcin Wadowita Grammar School for Boys. He holds this office through two terms, until March 20, 1938. The same year he co-directs a production of the *Nie-Boska Komedia* (*Un-Divine Comedy*) at the Catholic House. He plays the part of the Count Henry.

1937

February	School theatre production of Balladyna. Karol Wojtyła plays two roles: Kirkor and von Korstyn; he took over the second role after a schoolmate had to resign at the last moment.
June	*Sobótka*, based on Jan Kochanowski is put on in a Wadowice park by the school theatre.
July 5	He completes a military training camp in Hermanowice, obtaining the second rank.
September	He begins the graduating class (8th grade). There was a recital competition organized towards the end of that period. First place was taken by Halina Królikiewicz (later the known actress Halina Kwiatkowska) and Karol Wojtyła, who picked a very hard text for recitation – Norvid's Promethidion.

1938

February 1	Stanisław Wyspiański's play "Zygmunt August" is put on to celebrate the name day of Ignacy Mościcki, President of Poland. Karol Wojtyła plays the title role. Along with the Drama Club advisor, Kazimierz Foryś, he participated in directing the play and designing the scenery.
February 17	The League of the Catholic Youth put on a matinee at the "Sokół" sport society to celebrate an anniversary of the patriotic event of Poland being wedded to the sea. Karol Wojtyła gives a speech. The grammar school theatre also traveled to perform in Andrychów and Kalwaria. Student – actors attended theater in Cracow.
May 6	The Metropolitan, Prince Adam Stefan Sapiecha visits the Wadowice Marcin Wadowita Grammar School. Professor Szeliski and the student Karol Wojtyła both give speeches to welcome the archbishop.
May	Confirmation – he chooses Mr. Siłkowski, his friend's father to be his witness.
May 14	Maturity (graduation) exam. From the subjects tested, he receives the following grades: religion – excellent, Polish – excellent, Latin – excellent, Greek – excellent, German – excellent. He also obtained final grades for years VI to VIII. They went as follows: history along with contemporary Polish studies – excellent, basis of philosophy – excellent, physical education – excellent, and hygiene – excellent.
May 27	In the name of the graduating class, Karol Wojtyła thanks the professors assuring them that they will adhere to the instruction obtained at the school.
June 20 – July 17	Serves as a conscript in the 7th Battalion, 9th Company of the Youth Work Troop in Zubrzyca Górna.
July 12	He is authorized to wear the Youth Work Troop memorial badge.
Summer	Together with his father he moves to Cracow. They live at 10 Tyniecka St. in the Dębniki district, at the home of the Kaczorowski family, in two small rooms with a kitchen, on the ground floor.

A record of Karol Wojtyła's baptism
in the parish register book at the Church
of the Presentation of the Holiest Virgin Mary
in Wadowice.

The Church of the Pallotine Fathers (Collegium Marianum) on the outskirts of Wadowice.

The Kościuszko Square, formerly Rynek Zbożowy, it is currently a parking place in front of the Powiat Office. Photograph from the 1920's.

A wedding photograph of the Holy Father's parents, Emilia and Karol Wojtyła. The wedding ceremony took place in 1904 at the former garrison church of Saint Peter and Paul in Cracow.

The Wojtyłas with their oldest son Edmund,
photograph from 1908.

Karol Wojtyła's father in the uniform of a Polish legionary in 1915.

Army barracks on Lwowska Street, where the Pope's father managed the army office. In the foreground, monument of a legionnaire.

PAMIĄTKA PIERWSZEJ KOMUNJI ŚW.

Karol Wojtyła przyjął pierwszą Komunię
św. w kościele *parafjalnym* w *Wadowicach* dnia *25 maja* 1929

Karol Wojtyła's commemorative First Communion picture – also seen on the next photograph from the year 1929 – it stays at the Museum of the John Paul II Family Home in Wadowice.

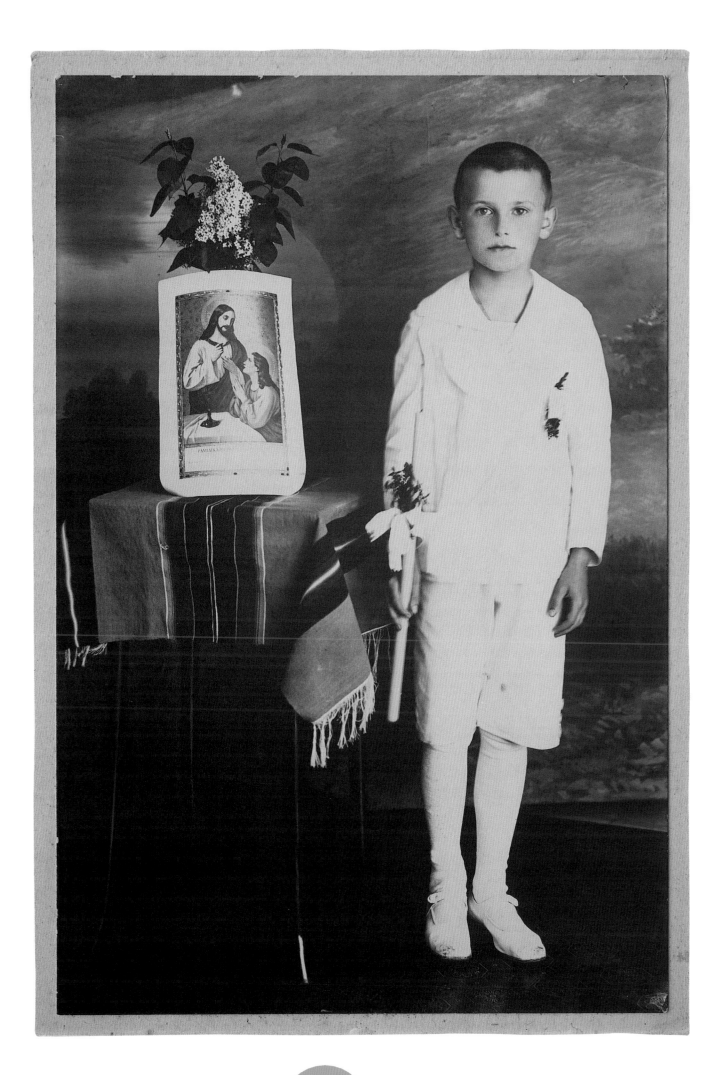

Karol as a grammar school first grader.

The late baroque cross at the entrance to the Wadowice Basilica of the Presentation of the Holiest Virgin Mary.

The Marcin Wadowita Grammar School, where Karol Wojtyła attended and passed his maturity exam in 1938. In front of the school stands a bust of the writer, Emil Zegadłowicz.

In the period between the Wars, this building housed an elementary school (which was attended by Karol Wojtyła) and the City Office. Currently, it is only the seat of the City Office.

w ogrodzie Szpitala w Bielsku

S. Käthe   S. Berta   S. Małgorzata
              Ja

A reverse of the next photograph;
an autograph of the Holy Father.

Little Karol Wojtyła (at the age of 10 or 11) with nurses in the garden of the Bielsko hospital, where His brother, Edmund, worked.

Karol Wojtyła as a grammar school
student (on the left), next to his father
and schoolmates in 1936.

At the Youth Work Troop camp (after his maturity exam) in Zubrzyca, where a road was being constructed. First on the left, Karol Wojtyła. Photograph from 1938.

Danuta Pukło-Gruszczyńska, Karol Wojtyła and Halina Królikiewicz-Kwiatkowska in a school play: *Ułani księcia Józefa* (*Prince Joseph Uhlans*).

Kazimiera Żakówna as Barbara Radziwiłłówna and Karol Wojtyła as Zygmunt August in Wyspiański's drama: *Zygmunt August* – performed by the grammar school theater (February 1938).

Mother…

M. Kremski   Kraków

…and son.

AS SAINT PETER'S SUCCESSOR

The Pope Needs Our Prayer

Recollections of a Catechist
s. Magdalena Strzelecka CFSN

The news spreads lightning fast through Poland and through the rest of the world. The smiling Pope, John Paul I, Albino Luciani, is dead after 33 days of pontificate. Our Polish cardinals leave for Rome, to attend the solemn funeral. Taking part in the prayers for the departed Pope is our cardinal, Karol Wojtyła. After the funeral, the whole Church prays for a new Pope to be chosen.

In our Wadowice parish church – under the invocation of the Presentation of the Holiest Virgin Mary – rosaries are being said. The church is filled with faithful. There are a lot of children taking an active part. On October 15, 1978, the sacristian, Alexander Spisak, says to me, "Maybe our cardinal, Karol Wojtyła will become Pope? There were journalists from Warsaw talking to the prelate Edward Zacher. They asked for information on the cardinal's life. From His earliest childhood."

The conclave in Rome is underway. We are listening to the radio updates for news of a Pope being chosen. At 5:30 p.m. we gather to say the rosary. Again the church is filled. There are a lot of children. Everyone is in deep prayer for the successful choosing St Peter's next successor.

Just prior to the blessing of the Most Holy Sacrament, the then – Wadowice curate, father Filip Piotrowski, comes out of the sacristy and raising his hands announces to the faithful, "Our Dearest Mother of Perpetual Help caused our Cracow cardinal, Karol Wojtyła, to be chosen Pope. The news was just on the radio". Incredible joy descended on the congregation. Shouts and cries of happiness. The sound of *Te Deum Laudamus* – We Praise You, Lord, rose up towards the heavens.

Nobody went home after the service. There was no end to the conversations, statements and surmises that most of Poland thought Karol Wojtyła the best candidate. It was getting dark. The sacristian wanted to lock up the church but found it to be impossible. The journalists began arriving in Wadowice late in the evening. They wanted to learn about the new Pope's roots, where was He born, where He lived, where is the font He was baptized at, are His relatives still around, what about His friends.... there was no end to the questions.

Radio, newspaper and TV reporters from the entire world crowded into father Zacher's sacristy for days to come. I remember that the last foreign reporter to show up was Chinese.

Wadowice also became a destination for pilgrims who came from all over Poland, fascinated by the Holy Father, wanting to see the place of His birth and the church He was baptized at. They visited all the places connected with His person, from His childhood up to the time He went to study in Cracow.

The festive inauguration of the Holy Father, John Paul II's pontificate was scheduled for October 22. A Wadowice delegation was sent to Rome. It consisted of father Michał Piosek (most senior of the curates), Zbigniew Siłkowski (Karol Wojtyła's best friend – they went to school together), Teresa and Andrzej Leń and the longtime Wadowice sacristian, Aleksander Spisak. Due to the huge numbers of pilgrims, who would never fit in the Vatican Basilica, the festive Mass took place in St Peter's Square.

The following morning, October 23, a special audience with the Holy Father was held for Poles, both those living in Poland and those from abroad. The audience took place in Paul VI's aula. On a podium, by a great cast sculpture of the Ascension, sat all the Polish bishops.

The Holy Father enters the aula at 4:20 p.m. He is accompanied by the prelate Juliusz Paetz from the papal antechamber and father Stanisław Dziwisz, His personal secretary. The appearance of the Pope's white silhouette gave rise to a storm of applause and shouts of "Long live the Pope!". When the crowd settled down, the Polish Primate, Cardinal Stefan Wyszyński said a few words and then the new Pope spoke.

My beloved brothers and sisters! Allow me to thank you for all the years of my life, for my schooling, priesthood and episcopate. How could have I predicted that they will all prepare me for Christ summoning me, on October 16, 1978, in the Sistine Chapel? From the point of view of this day, however, I must look back at all those who – not even realizing it – prepared me for this. My beloved parents, long departed, my Wadowice parish under the invocation of the Presentation of the Virgin Mary, my elementary and high schools, the Jagiellonian University, the Theology Department and the Seminary. What can I say about my great predecessor in the St Stanisław capital, Prince Cardinal Adam Stefan Sapiecha, about the great exile Archbishop Eugeniusz Baziak, about the bishops, priests, the many ardent shepherds, the wonderful professors and the exemplary monks and nuns. What about all the different laymen I've met throughout my life. About my schoolmates, friends from my university and seminary years, the workers at *Solvay* factory, intellectuals, writers, artists, people from so many professions, the married couples, students, the clerical circles, oasis, all the boys and girls trying to find sense in life with the Evangel in hand, sometimes even finding the path of clergy or monastic calling.

All this I carry in my heart and take with me: my beloved Cracow Church, this particular part of Christ's Church in Poland as well as of the history of our Homeland. The old Cracow – and the new one, new boroughs, new people, new neighborhoods, Nowa Huta, the struggle for new churches and parishes, new needs and conditions of evangelization, catechization and priesthood. All this was called up, along with me, to Saint Peter's capital. All this comprises an integral part of my soul, my experience, my faith and my love. It all spreads out over so many beloved places, to the Sanctuaries of Christ and those of His Mother. I want to mention Mogiła, Ludźmierz, Myślenice, Staniątki, Rychwałd and above all Kalwaria Zebrzydowska, with the paths I liked so much to stroll. In my eyes and in my heart I keep the sights of the entire Cracow region: Żywiec, Silesia, Podhale, the Beskids and the Tatras. This beloved land and Polish natural beauty I offer up to the Lord.

And most of all the people...

The Lord Jesus Christ be blessed!

"The Lord Jesus Christ be blessed", the Pope greets the people assembled in the aula. This Christian greeting can be heard in Polish at every general audience attended by Poles since the times of Pius XI (Achilles Ratti was the papal nuncio to Poland right after it regained its independence). What joy and pride when Paul VI added "*dzień dobry*" to it! Now this greeting is being said by the Polish Pope. This whole meeting is for Poles, in Polish... He started reading two farewell texts.... He was very moved. While saying His farewells to the Cracow Archdiocese, His voice broke. From then He really had to start reading. Maybe to compose himself or maybe to be with us sooner."

After blessing, together with the Polish bishops, the assembled pilgrims, the Holy Father went on to be among the Poles in the aula. There was an explosion of joy. The Pope recognized familiar faces, exchanged a few words with all. He went up to a Highlander delegation, which presented Him with a regional hat, a poleaxe and a carved trunk. It was a familiar and joyous occasion, full of happy shouts and singing. At one point the Holy Father said, "No one is to cry for me and everybody is to pray... I am counting on this and I am only staying here under these conditions..."

Joy, affection, tears and also sadness that cardinal Wojtyła will not be coming back to Cracow. Aleksander Spisak, when asked about his impressions, said, "it was an incredible experience, a funeral for the still-living". During the Polish meeting the Holy Father said that, God willing, He was planning to visit Poland in 1979. Our Homeland would be celebrating a Great Jubilee – the 900th Anniversary of the Death of St Stanisław, the Bishop of Cracow. Cardinal Wojtyła was preparing the Cracow Archdiocese for the celebration all through the 1972-1979 synod and wished to complete the task. This news was received with thundering applause. The people of Wadowice wondered among themselves, "Will the Holy Father visit His hometown?" Time will tell.

The Pope planned His first apostolic trip, to Mexico, for January 1979. An official notice arrives in Poland, saying that John Paul II is planning to visit His Homeland in the immediate future. Discussions between the Polish government and the Episcopate regarding the planning of the pilgrimage are already underway.

Soon afterwards, the people of Wadowice find out that the Holy Father will make a few hour stop there on His way to Oświęcim (Auschwitz). Preparations are being made to welcome our most distinguished and beloved Cardinal, Christ's Deputy and St Peter's successor.

The city council, prelate Zacher and members of other organizations form a committee to coordinate preparations for the Holy Father's visit to His hometown. The sisters teaching Sunday school are quickly preparing the children. Wadowice is the place of the Pope's birth, this is where He spent His childhood and youth, and therefore the children must be there to welcome Him back to His familiar parts.

First and foremost come spiritual preparations. Next in the order of importance is the care to prepare and decorate the place where the Pope is to meet with the townsfolk. The sisters dedicated many lessons to familiarize the children with John Paul II. There were plenty of subject to touch upon: who is the Pope we call the Holy Father? What is His role in the Church? Who was the first Pope? Why is the Church headquartered in Rome? How many Popes had there been? This is what the Sunday school students learned about. There was general interest in the matter and lessons were full of questions.

It would be difficult not to mention the meeting of kindergarten kids with reporters from the Polish state television. The kids were asked why the Pope was so important. The five and six-year-olds gave all sorts of answers. Each one wanted to say something and quite a ruckus was building up. One of the kindergarteners was raising his hand and trying to say something, but there was too much noise. When the kids quieted down a bit, little Janusz stood up and with all the seriousness a six-year-old can muster said: "the Pope is very important because He is God's assistant here on Earth". Hearing the child's words, the journalist commented, "these kids are smart". I have to add that these were kids from the excellent Kindergarten no. 2, run by Ms. Krystyna Zagórska. It is located in the building of the Sisters of Nazareth and in the period between the World Wars it was attended by the little Karol Wojtyła. Back then the word for kindergarten was "ochronka" – shelter.

At the same meeting a little boy named Waldek asked a foreign journalist: "what do you need all this stuff for? What do you do?". The journalist smiled and answered, "I'm going abroad and I want to show the kids there how you're experiencing your countryman becoming Pope."

Much prayer went along with the spiritual preparations. The Sunday school classroom was very near the church so we often went there with the children to pray for John Paul II. The need for such prayers was brought to our attention by a three-year-old named Piotruś who attended the lessons with his older siblings. He came up to my desk one day saying he wants to recite a poem. I asked the kids to quiet down and when we had silence little Piotruś said, "Keep in mind that I came from among you and therefore reserve for myself a special right to your hearts and your prayers". These were the words spoken by the Holy Father during His Polish audience following His inauguration on October 23. Little Piotruś heard these words and they must have made quite an impression on him seeing he memorized them so exactly.

John Paul II's arrival in Warsaw was planned for June 2, 1979. The visit to His hometown was scheduled for June 7. Preparations moved forward with full steam. A platform had to be erected in front of the church, streets and squares swept and brought to order. Some of the buildings in the town square had to be renovated too.

What was the attitude of the government – government of the Polish People's Republic?

They did not overtly interfere, but they did not show any great enthusiasm either. There were attempts to stir up panic in Wadowice and some other cities, not to let children out of schools in view of dangerous crowds that were sure to assemble. Still, it was possible to organize the children to meet with the Pope. The youngest kids from kindergartens were to assemble in the chapel of Our Lady of Perpetual Help. Those who received their first communion the past May, lined the main nave of the church. First-graders along with their parents welcomed the Pope at the "Skawa" sports stadium. Older youth and others who wanted to meet the Holy Father were to congregate on the square outside the church.

On October 2, around 10 a.m., the airplane carrying John Paul II to His Homeland touched down at Warsaw's Okęcie airport. All the church bells tolled. The ones in Wadowice sounded long and joyously. The inhabitants, with tears in their eyes, watched the television transmission as the Pope was being welcomed by the Cardinal Stefan Wyszyński, Polish bishops, clergy and dignitaries of the Polish People's Republic.

The days preceding the hometown visit were full of last minute preparations. For an event so anticipated, everything had to be perfect. In the early morning hours of Thursday, June 7, journalists – both Polish and foreign – started to descend on Wadowice. The inhabitants of surrounding towns also arrived to greet the Holy Father, hear His sermons and receive His blessing.

Traveling to Oświęcim (Auschwitz), the Pope stopped along the way at Kalwaria Zebrzydowska. At noontime, the helicopter carrying John Paul II landed at the "Skawa" stadium. After a short welcome, He entered a black, open-topped limousine and drove down Lwowska Street to the church square. Crowds of people accompanied Him the entire way. Older nuns and disabled children from our institution gathered in front of the Sisters of Nazareth house. The enthusiasm was tremendous and really impossible to describe – the Holy Father was blessing everyone, on both sides of the street.

In front of the church, on a beautifully decorated podium, the prelate Edward Zacher awaited the guest. He was a longtime local parish priest, Karol Wojtyła's religion teacher from His grammar school days, who taught and raised many priests and preachers. The Holy Father walked up onto the platform, raised His hand to greet the crowd and went down into the church. He walked up to the main altar between the rows of communion children. He patted them on the heads. A few kids even managed to kiss Him on the hand. After a short prayer before the Holiest Sacrament, He made His way to the Holy Family chapel, and up to the font at which He was baptized entering the Church community. Full of love and adoration, He kissed the font, thanking the Holy Trinity for the gift of being the Lord's child.

After the prayer the Holy Father talked to children. "What Virgin were you singing about just before?". "About the Mother of Jesus, about the Mother of God, about Mary our Mother", answered the children. "You sang about the Mother of Perpetual Help, who is always with us, at all times and never ceases to assist us", said the Holy Father. He saw the gifts the children had brought for Him and

June 7, 1979. Meeting of the Holy Father
with kindergarteners in the Chapel of Our
Lady of Perpetual Help. Children with their
religion teacher, sister Magdalena Strzelecka,
prepared a wonderful welcome for the Pope.

thanked them. Picking up a box filled with earth from Wadowice He said, "I am taking this box to Rome with me. I will put it under my pillow and at night I will sleep like if I were here."

Leaving the church, the Holy Father went back on the platform out front. There the prelate, Edward Zacher officially welcomed the guest:

"*Anuntio vobis geudium magnum: Habemus Papam!* I announce to you a great joy. We have a Pope!

These words have sounded for close to 2000 years from over the Bethlehem Manger – I announce to you a great joy: Jesus Christ – the Savior has been born. The Church repeats these words of joy to this day, proclaiming to the world a new Pope – Christ's assistant. These words sounded even more joyous this time around with the choosing of a Polish Pope. ...

There may be many reasons for our happiness. This is, of course, our countryman, student, friend, relative, but they are all small matters. First and foremost we are deeply moved and overjoyed because we know that standing here before us is the Deputy of Christ, our Savior.

We welcome Him with great affection and humility, stunned by the greatness of this Gift.

Holy Father! Great crowds sincerely and whole-heartedly welcomed Christ entering Jerusalem. Christ's enemies are hiding in the gates of houses. Wanting to silence the crowd, they approach Christ saying, "Why all this, why all the shouting. Tell them to be quiet." Christ answers them, "If the children and the crowds will not shout, then the stones shall shout for them. No one can extinguish Christian enthusiasm, there is supernatural strength in it." Christ said, "Have faith, I conquered the world!"

Holy Father! You have arrived among Your own, to Bethany, Your Fatherland, home, to Your countrymen, to the memories of Your youth – how beautiful they were. When God called You into His service, it was here You thanked Him solemnly for the gift of priesthood, in Your first Holy Mass, for the episcopate, for the metropolitan office, for the cardinalship and for the 50th anniversary of Your baptism.

I don't think that St John's words, "He came to be among his own and they wouldn't accept him", apply to us.

We wait for You with great longing, Holy Father! This is Your first mass as the Pope in Your hometown. We rush to Your feet to congratulate You and bring You our assurances of dedicating ourselves entirely to God and the Church. We cry out: Blessed be he who goes in the name of the Lord...

We swear to last at Your side in the service of Christ, the Savior of man."

At this time the Holy Father spoke:

"*Deeply moved, I have arrived today to this city, the city of my birth – to the parish where I was baptized and accepted to the community of Christ's Church – to the environment, I developed powerful ties with through eighteen years of my life, from the time of my birth up to graduating high school.*

When I look here on this square, nearly every detail connects me to memories of the earliest period of my life.

I would like to thank you for the welcome I received and to wholeheartedly greet you myself. A lot of time has passed since I lived in Wadowice and things have changed a great deal. I would, therefore, like to greet the new inhabitants, while always keeping in mind the old: the generation coming of age in the period between the World Wars. I am coming back with my thoughts and my heart not only to the house I was born at, right near the church,

but also to the elementary school, here in the town square, and the Marcin Wadowita Grammar School, both of which I attended.

As far as I know, there are more high schools in Wadowice today. Back then, the Marcin Wadowita Grammar School, later joined by the Michalina Mościcka Girls' School had to cover a very large territory. We had schoolmates from Kalwaria, Andrychów, from Zator and from Sucha, towns that did not have grammar schools of their own. Now they all have them. I also remember that this old and deserving Wadowice grammar school, one of the oldest in this part of Poland, celebrated its 100th anniversary the same year we celebrated a millennium of Christianity in Poland. I remember this. In my thoughts and in my heart I am returning also to my friends from elementary and even more from grammar school. More, because it lasted longer. I am from a generation that still attended eight-year grammar schools. Together with my generation I am thinking back to our parents, our teachers and to our professors. Very few of them are still alive. Some of my contemporaries, especially those who graduated with me in 1938 are still here today – those I would like greet with particular affection. I would also like to thank them because, when the whole new Pope matter came up on October 16 of last year and journalists descended on Wadowice, they – and especially prelate Zacher – spoke well of me. Better than I deserve. I also think about all my other friends and classmates who scattered all through Poland and the world – I think that they too will find out about our meeting.

It is a fact well known what great influence the earliest years, and then youth have on the development of one's personality and character. These are the years which link me inseparably with Wadowice, which back then bore the proud title – "Royal Free City of Wadowice"... and also with this whole area. With the Skawa River, the Beskid mountain range. This is why I wanted to come here and together with you thank the Lord for all the good I experienced here. I turn my prayers to many of the departed, starting with my parents, my older brother and a sister I never knew because she died before I was born. Their memory is yet another thing which binds me to this city.

As one man to another I would like to express my gratitude to the prelate, Edward Zacher, who was my religion professor at the Wadowice grammar school and who spoke at my first masses as a priest, as a bishop and as a cardinal, right here in the Wadowice church. He spoke again here at this new stage in my life, which cannot be explained by anything else but by boundless Divine Mercy and uncommon care of the Mother of God, Mother of Perpetual Help.

When I look back, I see how the path of my life through this place, through this parish, and through my family, leads me to one place. To the baptismal font of the Wadowice parish church. It was at this font, that on June 20, 1920, I was accepted to the grace of being God's child and to the faith of my Savior and to the community of His Church. The first time I solemnly kissed this font,

50th anniversary of the prelate, Edward Zacher's priesthood, a long time catechist of Karol Wojtyła. On June 26, 1977, Cardinal Karol Wojtyła placed a symbolic laurel wreath on His former professor's head.

as the archbishop of Cracow, during the celebration of one-thousandth anniversary of Poland's baptism. Then, as the prelate recounted to us, I did it again as a cardinal, on the 50th anniversary of my own baptism. Today, I kissed it for the third time, coming from Rome as St Peter's successor.

I could once again gaze at the face of the Mother of Perpetual Help in the painting of Her, here in Wadowice. I want to ask you all to keep praying for me in front of this image.

I would also like to give my sincere greetings to all the nuns gathered here. In my times there were only the Sisters of Nazareth here; I even used to come around their way, when I was at the age they still call a man "kid". I know that today there are also the Sisters of St Albert, and I see the Sisters of the Presentation as well, but I think they just came here on a pilgrimage... My sincere greetings to the priests. To all the priests, those from Wadowice and those visiting. Many priests came through Wadowice. It was a large parish and they always had a number of them here. With great affection I remember all the local priests, now departed. Especially the late father prelate Leonard Prochownik, local parish priest for many years, my departed religion instructors, father Pawela, father Rospond and father Włodyga – God rest their souls. I remember – I remember them all.

As far as the orchestra is concerned – Wadowice has an excellent orchestra. And a civilian one at that. There was a wonderful orchestra here before the war too. The Twelfth Infantry Regiment Orchestra, something the younger generation knows nothing about. But we, the older ones know: The Wadowice Region Regiment, 12th Infantry Regiment...

At the end, my beloved ones, I want to ask you to keep praying for me here in front of Our Lady of Perpetual Help, because the Pope – more than anyone else –is in particular need of perpetual help."

The assembled crowd received the Holy Father's speech with tumultuous ovation. After giving His apostolic blessing, the Pope went to dine and rest at the presbytery. It was there that He met with Ms. Helena Szczepańska, a retired teacher, who as the Wojtyła's neighbor often babysat the young Karol when His mother had to run errands.

The guest departed from His hometown. His helicopter took off from the stadium, punctually at 3 p.m., bound for Oświęcim. There, the Holy Father celebrated mass and prayed at the bunker where St Maksymilian Kolbe was starved to death.

Wadowice was under impression of the Papal visit for days to come. The Holy Father's Homeland Pilgrimage was nearing its end. On June 10, a huge ceremony took place at the Błonia meadow in Cracow – the celebration of the great Jubilee of the 900th Anniversary of the Martyrdom of St Stanisław, the Bishop. Many people from Wadowice attended. They cherished in they hearts the words, the Holy Father spoke during this mass,

Before I leave from here, I am asking you to accept this whole spiritual heritage – called Poland, with faith, hope, and with love – the same one that Christ instills in us during the holy baptism:
– for you to never fall into doubt, get weary or discouraged,
– for you never to sever the roots we stem from. This I ask you.
– for you to trust, even in spite of all your weaknesses to always seek spiritual assistance with Him, which is where so many generations of our fathers and mothers found it,
– for you to never forsake Him, never to lose the freedom in spirit He liberates in man,
– for you never to scorn this Love, the greatest thing of all, expressed through the Cross, and without which human life would have neither roots nor sense.
I ask this of you for the sake of memory and through the powerful intercession of Our Lady from Jasna Góra and from all Her other Polish sanctuaries.

Prayer at the church of his childhood.

Pages 42-43: Meeting with His townsfolk from Wadowice at the square in front of the church, June 7, 1979 at noontime.

GRATEFUL
TO GOD

August 14,
1991, prayer
in front
of the image
of Our Lady of
Perpetual Help.

Wadowice's Lady

The Cult of Our Lady of Perpetual Help

The image of Our Lady of Perpetual Help was most likely created in 12th century in Crete and belongs to the eastern group of religious paintings. Stolen by the Knights of the Teutonic Order, it was brought to Rome and put in care of the Augustinian Friars. Between the years of 1499 to 1798 it remained at St Matthew Church on Esquilino Hill where it was surrounded with great veneration and worship by the faithful. After the renovation conducted by a Pole, Leopold Nowotny, the image of Our Lady was crowned on June 23, 1867 in Rome and today it remains at the Church of St Alphonsus. Through the intercession of Our Lady of Perpetual Help pilgrims received numerous graces, which helped to spread the cult of this image.

The origins of the worship of Our Lady of Perpetual Help in Wadowice are related to missions which took place between October 16-27, 1897 and were led by the Redemptorist Fathers, known for spreading the Marian cult. The image in Wadowice is painted on 190x80 cm canvas and it is a copy of the picture from St Alphonsus Church in Rome. It represents the Madonna holding the Baby in Her left arm, while Jesus places His little hands in Her right hand. On the left side of the picture there is Gabriel, holding the cross, a symbol of suffering, and on the right side there is Michael holding a vessel with a sponge and a spear – symbols of Christ's Passion. The picture prompts the faithful to deep reflection on the role of Church's Mother, who embraces Her son Jesus and all the people with Her goodness and love. She makes us persist in the hope that in turning to Her, we can always count on Her help.

The magnitude of Mary's worship in the Wadowice Church is expressed by the numerous votive offerings such as golden hearts, crosses, necklaces, and ornamental pectoral plates. There is also a papal medal of John Paul II and President Lech Wałęsa's cup.

On June 16, 1999, during the pilgrimage to his Homeland, the Holy Father solemnly crowned the miraculous painting of Our Lady of Perpetual Help. The crowns were made from votive offerings such as wedding rings, gold earrings, chainlets and rings. Karol Wojtyła often prayed before the image of Wadowice's Lady and therefore, a commemorative plate with the words of the Holy Father, "I ask all of you to embrace me with unceasing prayer in front of this Mother" was placed in one of the chapel's walls.

The Świętokrzyska chapel, with the image of Our Lady of Perpetual Help surrounded with great veneration by the inhabitants of Wadowice and neighboring communities.

August 14, 1991, second visit of the Holy
Father in His hometown. Consecration
of a new church under the invocation
of St Peter the Apostle – a votive offering
for choosing a Pole to the St Peter's See
and for saving His life after the assassination.

The consecration ceremony of the new church under the invocation of St Peter the Apostle in Wadowice.

The Holy Father, John Paul II along with the Cracow Metropolitan, Cardinal Franciszek Macharski, consecrate the church.

The statue of John Paul II standing watch over St Peter the Apostle Church.

St Peter's Church was built by the Cracow Archdiocese in gratitude for saving the life of John Paul II after the assassination attempt on May 13th 1981.

Modernity and harmony are the main features of both the exterior and interior of St Peter the Apostle Church.

Near "Golgotha" Our Lady of Fatima encourages to say the Rosary.

"Golgotha." A park with the Way of the Cross created on the 25th anniversary of the pontificate of John Paul II, and consecrated by Cardinal Franciszek Macharski, the Metropolitan Archbishop of Cracow, on August 13th 2003.

Meeting of the
Holy Father with
the sick in the
square next to
the new church.

Second pilgrimage to Wadowice (1991).
The Holy Father at the historic baptismal font
at which He was baptized on June 20, 1920.

The church interior after redecoration.

Prelate Kazimierz Suder, back then, a parish priest of the Church of the Presentation of the Holiest Virgin Mary, informs the Holy Father about the restoration of the Świętokrzyska chapel.

The late baroque main altar of the parish church. In the mid-nineteenth century its invocation was changed from the All Saints to the Presentation of the Holiest Virgin Mary.

Pages 64-65:
Skawa River flows from the mountains and constitutes a natural boundary of Wadowice.

MANY YEARS
HAVE PASSED

The prayer of
John Paul II was
His dialogue
with God.

The "Skawa" Sports Club Stadium, landing
place of the Papal helicopter. Third visit of the
Holy Father in Wadowice (June 16, 1999).

Lwowska Street. Papal suite on their way from
the stadium to the Basilica.

Every time John Paul II visited his hometown, the faithful were overcome with deep emotion, great enthusiasm and hope.

Holy Father accompanied by the parish priest, prelate Jakub Gil, in front of the altar built especially for the Pope's visit. On the left is Cardinal Franciszek Macharski.

John Paul II standing at the open-air altar in front of the Basilica in Wadowice in June 1999. Next to him, Archbishop Piero Marini, the papal master of ceremonies for liturgical celebrations and one of the closest people to the Pope. On the right, the Secretary of the Vatican State, Cardinal Angelo Sodano.

Next page:
The Papal altar was situated between Jonh Paul II's family home and the Basilica.

A 160-student interschool choir managed by Paweł Jarosz sang many beautiful songs.

Here, in this town, in Wadowice, everything started. The life started here, and school started here, studies started here and theater. And priesthood started here.
(John Paul II, Wadowice 1999).

The town of my childhood, for love of the house – my family home and the house of the Lord – I will pray for your good!
(John Paul II, Wadowice 1999).

First communion children – Agnieszka
Lemrfeld and Tomek Fila pass the crowns,
which will be placed on the image of Our
Lady of Perpetual Help by the Holy Father.
The crowns were made from golden jewelry
presented as offerings by people from
Wadowice. Our Lady's crown bears the Papal
heraldic arms and the crown of the Baby
– the Wadowice coat of arms.

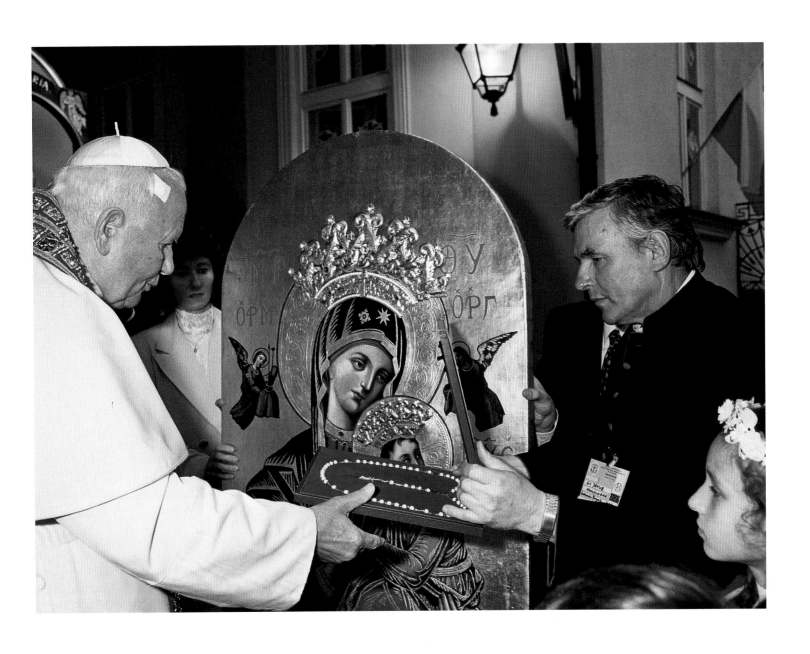

After the coronation, the Holy Father
presented a votive offering of a golden rosary,
which is received by the prelate Jakub Gil.

Next page:
The Holy Father praying
at the main altar of the Basilica.

This extraordinarily well-done bust of John Paul II welcomes thousands of pilgrims arriving from all over the world to visit the great Pope's church of His childhood.

Following the Holy Father's visit, the altar was not disassembled until after September 14. Pilgrims arriving in Wadowice placed flowers at the Papal altar and prayed at the cross, which was brought for John Paul II's visit by the faithful from the 10 km distant Witanowice.

After the destruction of communist times, Wadowice Market Square is now impressive and picturesque.

The corner building on the left (of the Market Square) is the home of the Wojtyła family: the entrance was at the rear. Now, the ground floor houses a superb bookshop specializing in books devoted to John Paul II.

Celebrations of the 25th anniversary of John
Paul II's pontificate, October 16th 2003

84th birthday of the Holy Father, May 18th
2004. The parade of Fire Brigade Orchestras
from various regions of Poland.

A historic
(about 200
years)
Wadowice
cemetery, where
among others,
many people
close to the
Holy Father
are buried.

May 18, 1984. A solemn Holy Mass celebrated by the Cracow Metropolitan, Franciszek Macharski on the occasion of the Holy Father's birthday and the opening of a museum called: "The John Paul II Family Home".

Chapel of The Crucified Christ in the right aisle of the Basilica.

RECOLLECTIONS
OF THE FAMILY HOME

Previous page: A wooden Church of St Erasmus in Barwałd, located on the route from Wadowice to Kalwaria. Karol Wojtyła often prayed in this church, in front of the 16th century image of Our Lady, which enjoys a remarkable cult.

And when I looked out of the window, I saw on the church's wall a sun-dial with the inscription: *Time passes by, eternity waits.* (John Paul II, Wadowice 1999).

On the left:
The parish
church, raised
to the rank
of basilica in
1992, next to
it the Catholic
House, where
towards the
end of 1930's,
Karol Wojtyła
performed
in a school
theatre.

On the right:
the family home
of the Wojtyłas';
their flat was
located on the
second floor.

An interior of the John Paul II Family Home Museum at 7 Kościelna Street. On the photograph, the room where Karol Wojtyła was born.

Just near the former entrance door was the Wojtyłas' kitchen.

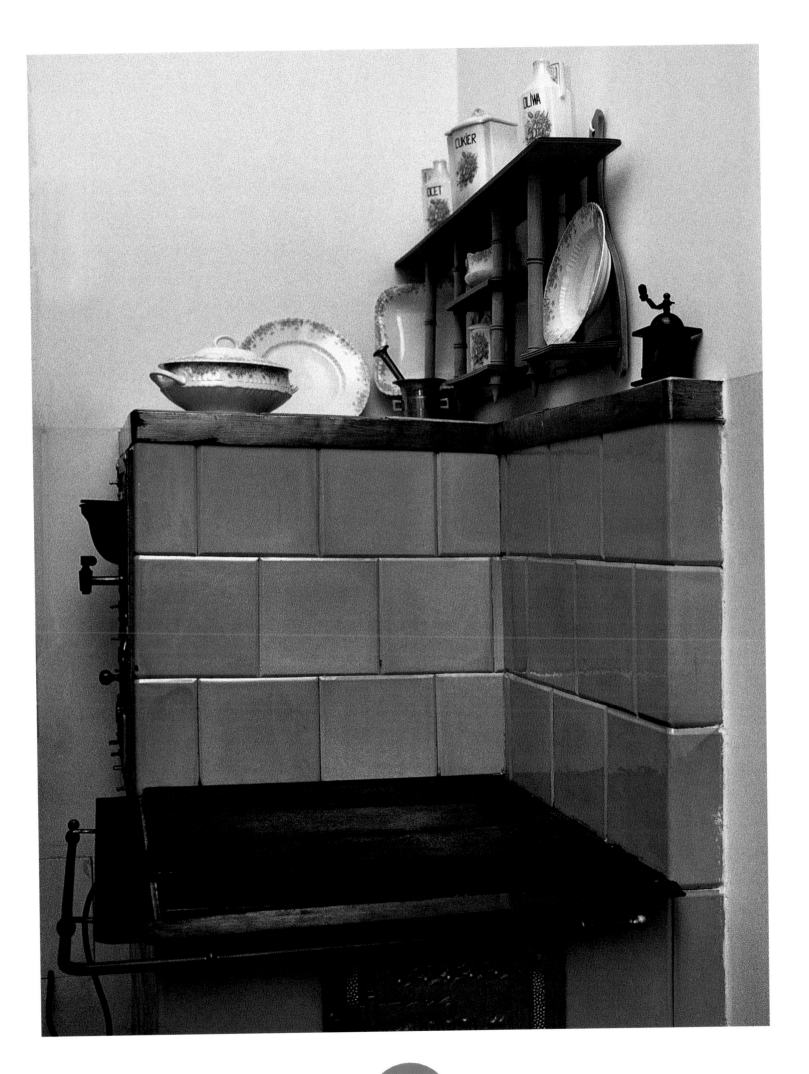

In this room of the museum, many exhibits documenting the pontificate of John Paul II have been gathered.

A diary entry, grammar school student Karol Wojtyła
wrote in the diary of his friend Danuta Pukło:

There are such holy, bright days
– the soul brightly goes to frolic
she dreams entangled in happiness
and it seems to her that 'till life's end
she won't free herself from these golden snares
– 'cause entangled in happiness she dreams
But later....
such black moments of suffering and fear
will descend on life's crossroads
and linger and cover with autumn
and torment the soul...
– – but they too shall pass...

KW.
25.V.1938

Są takie ciche, jasne dni
– obloką na gody idą jasną
o szczęścia oplotach śni
i zdaje się, że po życia kres oczów
nie wybierze już że szczęścia złoty wątki
– bo w szczęścia oplotach jasnych śni –

A potem . . . . .
przyjdą takie czarne chwile męki,
                              trwogi
przyjdą na życia rozwoje, rozdroży
i staną słupem, i zgromią pierwej
i drogą duszy . . .
        – – lecz i te się przemienią . . .

                              RW.
                    _____

                              25. I. 1881.

UNIWERSYTET JAGIELLOŃSKI W KRAKOWIE
WYDZIAŁ TEOLOGICZNY

L. 284/48

DYPLOM
MAGISTRA TEOLOGII

Ks. Karol W O J T Y Ł A,

urodzony dnia 18 maja 1920 roku w Wadowicach, wojew.krakowskie

odbył przepisane studia xx filozoficzno-teologiczne (tajne) w Seminarium Duchownym Krakowskim w latach 1942 - 1945, które na podstawie uchwały Rady Wydziału Teologicznego Uniwersytetu Jagiellońskiego z dnia 16.II. 1945 r. zaliczono do studiów uniwersyteckich, na Wydziale Teologicznym U.J.w latach 1945-1945/46, oraz w Instytucie "Angelicum" w Rzymie w r.1946/47

od roku akad. — — — do roku akad. _____ i zdał następujące egzaminy:

z filozofii chrześcijańskiej i historii filozofii . . . z wynikiem bardzo dobrym

z nauk biblijnych Nowego Zakonu . . . . z wynikiem celującym

z nauk biblijnych Starego Zakonu. . . . . z wynikiem celującym

z historii Kościoła katolickiego . . . . . . z wynikiem celującym

z teologii fundamentalnej (apologetyki) . . . z wynikiem celującym

z teologii dogmatycznej . . . . z wynikiem celującym

z teologii moralnej ogólnej i szczegółowej . . . z wynikiem celującym

z prawa kanonicznego . . . . z wynikiem celującym

z teologii pastoralnej z liturgiką i homiletyką . . z wynikiem celującym

z pedagogiki, katechetyki i metodyki . . . . . z wynikiem bardzo dobrym

oraz przedstawił z wynikiem bardzo dobrym pracę magisterską na temat

"Pojęcie środka zjednoczenia duszy z Bogiem w nauce św.Jana od Krzyża".

Wobec tego Rada Wydziału Teologicznego Uniwersytetu Jagiellońskiego na wniosek Komisji Egzaminacyjnej nadaje Księdzu K a r o l o w i   W O J T Y L E stopień

MAGISTRA TEOLOGII

jako dowód zakończenia studiów uniwersyteckich

W Krakowie, dnia 24 listopada 1948 r.

REKTOR   DZIEKAN

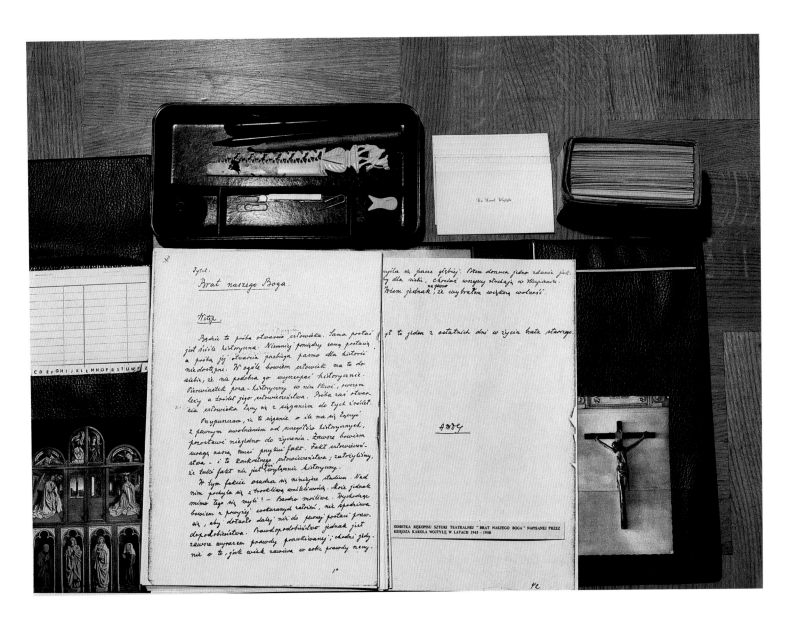

The drama, *Brat naszego Boga* (*The Brother of Our God*) – first page of the manuscript.

Among the museum's exhibits, also an M.A. diploma. Karol Wojtyła receives excellent grades in eight subjects and very good grades in two subjects. The M.A. thesis defended with a very good grade.

A rucksack used by Karol Wojtyła when walking in the mountains and kayaking on the Mazury Lakes, first as a bishop, and then as the Cracow Metropolitan. On the rucksack is a bishop's breviary.

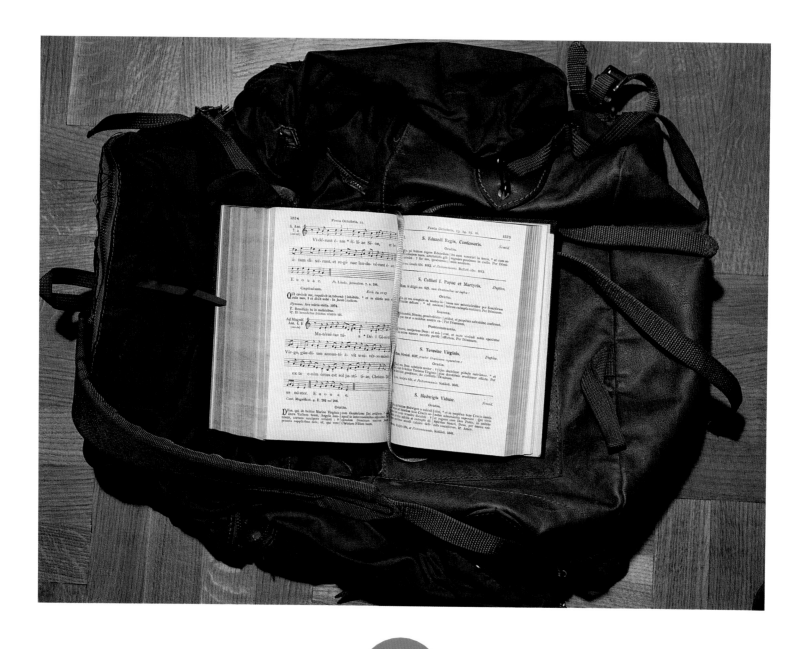

Bishop and then archbishop, Karol Wojtyła, skied the Beskidys and Tatras slopes using these shoes and skies.

A rosary from sister Lucia from Fatima presented to the Holy Father. It is currently in the John Paul II Museum in Wadowice (just as the other exhibits presented here on the photographs).

A chalice (masterly crafted in gold and ivory) and a paten, a gift to the museum, used by the Holy Father during the Holy masses in His private chapel at the Vatican.

A rosary on which the Holy Father prayed for years on first Saturdays of a month at the studio of the Vatican Radio; these programs were broadcasted worldwide.

A scapular, which Karol Wojtyła received as child from father Sylwester, a Discalced Carmelite at the St Joseph Church in Wadowice. Karol Wojtyła wore it on his chest for dozens of years.

Seven Centuries of Wadowice

Short History

The first historical mention of this place comes from 1327. In 1430 Wadowice received city rights. In 1445 it became a part of the Duchy of Oświęcim, and later the Duchy of Zator. In 1494, after the death of Prince Janusz IV, King Zygmunt I Stary incorporated the Duchy of Zator into Poland. Despite numerous privileges, Wadowice, which was located far from the main trade routes, developed slowly.

As a result of the First Partition of Poland in 1772 the town was annexed into Austria. Between 1819 and 1867 Wadowice was the seat of Starostwo (a historic administrative district), and since 1867 – of Powiat. In 1888 the town became joined by rail with Kalwaria Zebrzydowska and Bielsko. In 1918, after Poland regained its independence, Wadowice was returned to the Homeland.

During World War II, the Skawa River, flowing through Wadowice became the border between the Reich and General Government. In 1940 the Nazis arrested and transported to concentration camps scores of local intellectuals, activists of social and workers' movements. During the Nazi occupation, the Wadowice area was a region of Home Army (the Polish underground army of the Resistance Movement) activity – mainly acts of sabotage.

The courses of the town's history were impressed on the centrally located church in which Our Lady of Perpetual Help is venerated. The oldest mention of the church comes from the year 1325. According to the church's records, a wooden church burned down a century later and a new, gothic church made of brick was erected in its place in 1440. The church was reconstructed numerous times, following fires and therefore various architectonic styles can be observed there. The chancel comes from the 15th century, the nave with aisles and tower were constructed between 1791 – 98. The remaining parts are from the 19th and 20th centuries. In the 19th century a renowned Cracovian architect, Tomasz Pryliński, gave the church façade its final shape. During the bombing of the town on January 24, 1945 structure of the church and the chapel of Our Lady suffered damage.

Classicistic houses from 1840 were preserved in the town center.

There are some famous people associated with Wadowice.

Marcin Jan Kępa Wadowita (1567-1641), a theologian and ascetical writer, Piarist, professor and rector of Cracow Academy, author of numerous, important theological works. He came from a poor family. He became dean of the Theology Department and was an esteemed academic teacher. He supported the sick and poor. He founded a hospital and a school in Wadowice.

Józef Kalinowski, Father Rafał (1835-1907). He led the January Uprising in Lithuania, a member of the National Government during the January Uprising, exiled to Siberia. After his return from Siberia in 1877 he joined the Order of the Discalced Carmelites. He founded and built a church and monastery of Discalced Carmelites in Wadowice. He was beatified in 1983 and canonized in 1991 by the Holy Father, John Paul II.

Blessed Father Alfons Mazurek (1891 – 1944), Discalced Carmelite. In 1920 – 1930 he was a form master and a teacher in the Lower Seminary in Wadowice. He is the example of fidelity to God and apostolate devotion.

Emil Zegadłowicz (1888-1941), a poet and novelist, co-founder of the Beskid Mały writers' group – "Czartak".

Yet still, the most important person in the whole history of the town is undoubtedly Karol Wojtyła, who on October 16, 1978 r, after his election to The Holy See adopted the name of John Paul II. The Pope visited his hometown in 1979, 1991 and 1999.

The Monastery of the Discalced Carmelite Friars, in a background on the left is the St Joseph Church, with a monument of St Rafał Kalinowski the builder of these premises.

The Monastery of the Discalced Carmelite Order of Friars was Karol Wojtyła's favourite place to go to when he was a middle school student. On the left, the statue of St Joseph; on the right, the monastery buildings with St Joseph's Church.

Pages 114-115:
Basilica's interior
(1980's).

On the left:
Saint
Nepomucene
in Barwałd.

On the right:
The Crucified
Christ
– a sculpture
from the nearby
Kalwaria.

A characteristic Wadowice area landscape.

A view of Kalwaria from the direction of Lanckorona, the sanctuary can be seen in the distance, on the hill.

Kalwaria Zebrzydowska Sanctuary is 13 km away from Wadowice. Karol Wojtyła used to come here as a pilgrim from His childhood times up to the time he was pope. Following his footsteps, the sisters of Mother Teresa of Calcutta (the Missionaries of Charity), arrive in Kalwaria.

The sisters from India coming back from the Kalwaria Golgotha to the Basilica.

Next page:
The panorama of Kalwaria and the Beskidy Mountains.

LAMENT

On the left:
the funeral
ceremony
of Pope
John Paul II
celebrated by
Cardinal Joseph
Ratzinger,
now Pope
Benedict XVI.
The whole
world was in
mourning after
the death of
the Wadowice
Pope...

On the night after the death of their beloved John Paul II, thousands in Wadowice prayed for and to their great fellow countryman. It was immediately obvious that the announcement of the Pope's sainthood is just a matter of time. "Santo subito!," ("Immediate Sainthood!") chanted the faithful during the funeral ceremony in Rome's St Peter's Square.

In the evening on May 17th 2005 Wadowice
and the whole of Poland celebrated John
Paul II's 85th birthday with due ceremony.
He was no doubt watching from a window
in the House of The Lord. In the photograph,
Edyta Geppert performs against the
background image of the miraculous painting
of Our Lady of Kalwaria.

Iwona Schymalla and Grzegorz Miśtal, television viewers' favourites, led this wonderful birthday concert "in memoriam."

Outstanding Polish artists sang on stage: amongst others, Krzysztof Krawczyk (who performed "The Lord is My Shepherd" beautifully), Anna Maria Jopek, Marta Bizoń, Andrzej and Jacek Zieliński and Grzegorz Turnau. The photograph shows Justyna Steczkowska singing.

Santo subito! (Immediate Sainthood!) – with the silent invocation floating in the air during the concert, John Paul II was the greatest listener, gently looking down on all the people from His window in the House of God.

Wadowice, the beginning of the
20th century, the 3rd of May Polish

*The authors wish to thank the Museum
of John Paul II Family Home in Wadowice
for help in preparing this album.*

Consultation
sr. Magdalena Strzelecka CFSN

German translation
Jolanta Lenard
Adam Sosnowski

English translation
Eunika Bogucka-Jamka
Aneta Ptak (pages: 41, 53-57, 60, 67,
        70-73, 83-87, 113, 122-133)
Language consultant
Tomasz Chwaja

French Translation
Anna Garycka

Italian Translation
Jolanta Kornecka
Stefano Deflorian

DTP:
"Biały Kruk" Studio:
Wojciech Bartkowski
Sebastian Stachowski

Historical photography
Archives of the "Family Home of John Paul II"

Photograph on page 30 (left)
Kazimierz Koczur
...on page 36
Arturo Mari

Proof-reading
Bogdana Kłeczkowa

Publishing co-operation
Medienboerse

Printed in Czech Republic

Biały Kruk Sp. z o.o.
ul. Szwedzka 38
PL 30-324 Kraków
tel. +48 12/ 260 32 40, 260 32 90
e-mail: biuro@bialykruk.pl
www.bialykruk.pl

Second Edition (extended)
Kraków 2005

ISBN 83-88918-85-0